ROBERT LOUIS STEVENSON'S THOUGHTS ON WALKING

BY

ROBERT LOUIS STEVENSON

British Library Cataloguing-in-Publication Data
A catalogue record for this book is available from the
British Library

Contents

Robert Louis Stevenson

Robert Lewis Balfour Stevenson was born in Edinburgh, Scotland in 1850. Aged seventeen, he enrolled at the University of Edinburgh, but he was a disinterested student whose bohemian lifestyle detracted from his studies, and four years later, in April of 1971, he declared his decision to pursue a life of letters. A keen traveller, Stevenson became involved with a number of European literary circles, and had his first paid piece, an essay entitled 'Roads', published in 1873.

Stevenson suffered from various ailments and a "weak chest" for the whole of his life, and spent much of his adult years searching for a place of residence suitable to his state of ill health. In 1880, he married Fanny Van de Grift, and they moved between France, Britain and California together. It was during these years that Stevenson produced much of his best-known work – *Treasure Island,* in 1883, *The Strange Case of Dr Jekyll and Mr Hyde,* in 1886, and *Black Arrow,* in 1888. Following the death of his father in 1887, Stevenson devoted his later years to travels in the Pacific. During the late 1880s, he spent extended periods of time in both the Hawaiian and Samoan Islands, befriending many native and colonial leaders of the day and writing a number of accounts of his travels. In 1890 he purchased a 400-acre tract of land in Samoa, where he would remain for the rest of his life.

By 1894, still suffering from various ailments, he fell into a state of depression, and in December of that year, while straining to open a bottle of wine, he collapsed, most likely from a cerebral haemorrhage. A few hours later he was dead, aged just 44. Stevenson remains highly popular to this day, and is ranked the 26th most translated author in the world.

THE
LORE OF THE WANDERER
AN ANTHOLOGY OF THE OPEN-AIR

WALKING TOURS

IT must not be imagined that a walking tour, as some would have us fancy, is merely a better or worse way of seeing the country. There are many ways of seeing landscape quite as good; and none more vivid, in spite of canting dilettanti, than from a railway train. But landscape on a walking tour is quite accessory. He who is indeed of the brotherhood does not voyage in quest of the picturesque, but of certain jolly humours—of the hope and spirit with which the march begins at morning, and the peace and spiritual repletion of the evening's rest. He cannot tell whether he puts his knapsack on, or takes it off, with more delight. The excitement of the departure puts him in key for that of the arrival. Whatever he does is not only a reward in itself, but will be further rewarded in the sequel; and so pleasure leads on to pleasure in an endless chain. It is this that so few can understand; they will either be always lounging or always at five miles an hour; they do not play off the one against the other, prepare all day for the evening, and all evening for the next day. And, above all, it is here that your overwalker fails of comprehension. His heart rises against those who drink their curaçoa in liqueur glasses, when he himself can swill it in a brown John. He will not believe that the flavour is more delicate in the smaller dose. He will not believe that to walk this unconscionable distance is merely to stupefy and brutalise himself, and come to his inn, at night, with a sort of frost on his five wits, and a starless night of darkness in his spirit. Not for him the mild luminous evening of the temperate walker! He has nothing left of man but a physical need for bedtime and a double nightcap; and even his pipe, if he be a smoker, will be savourless and disenchanted. It is the fate of such an one to take twice as much trouble as is needed to obtain happiness, and miss the happiness in the end; he is the man of the proverb, in short, who goes further and fares worse.

Now, to be properly enjoyed, a walking tour should be gone upon alone. If you go in a company, or even in pairs, it is no longer a walking tour in anything but name; it is something else and more in the nature of a picnic. A walking tour should be gone upon alone, because freedom is of the essence; because you should be able to stop and go on, and follow this way or that, as the freak takes you; and because you must have your own pace, and neither trot alongside a champion walker, nor mince in time with a girl. And then you must be open to all impressions and let your thoughts take colour from what you see. You should be as a pipe for any wind to play upon. "I cannot see the wit," says Hazlitt, "of walking and talking at the same time. When I am in the country I wish to vegetate like the country,"—which is the gist of all that can be said upon the matter. There should be no cackle of voices at your elbow, to jar on the meditative silence of the morning. And so long as a man is reasoning he cannot surrender himself to that fine intoxication that comes of much motion in the open air, that begins in a sort of dazzle and sluggishness of the brain, and ends in a peace that passes comprehension.

During the first day or so of any tour there are moments of bitterness, when the traveller feels more than coldly towards his knapsack, when he is half in a mind to throw it bodily over the hedge and, like Christian on a similar occasion, "give three leaps and go on singing." And yet it soon acquires a property of easiness. It becomes magnetic; the spirit of the journey enters into it. And no sooner have you passed the straps over your shoulder than the lees of sleep are cleared from you, you pull yourself together with a shake, and fall at once into your stride. And surely, of all possible moods, this, in which a man takes the road, is the best. Of course, if he *will* keep thinking of his anxieties, if he *will* open the merchant Abudah's chest and walk arm-in-arm with the hag—why, wherever he is, and whether he walk fast or slow, the chances are that he will not be happy. And so much the more shame to himself! There are perhaps thirty men setting forth at that same hour, and I would lay a large wager there is not another dull face among the thirty. It would be a fine thing to follow, in a coat of darkness, one after another of these wayfarers, some summer morning, for the first few miles upon the road. This one, who walks fast, with a keen look in his eyes, is all concentrated in his own mind; he is up at his loom, weaving and weaving, to set the landscape to words. This one peers about, as he goes, among the grasses; he waits by the canal to watch the dragon-flies; he leans on the gate of the pasture, and cannot look enough upon the complacent kine. And here comes another, talking, laughing, and gesticulating to himself. His face changes from time to time, as indignation flashes from his eyes or anger clouds his forehead. He is composing articles, delivering orations, and conducting the most impassioned interviews, by the way. A little farther on, and it is as like as not he will begin to sing. And well for him, supposing him to be no great master in that art, if he stumble across no stolid peasant at a corner; for on such an occasion, I scarcely know which is the more troubled, or whether it is worse to suffer the confusion of your troubadour, or the unfeigned alarm of your clown. A sedentary population, accustomed, besides, to the strange mechanical bearing of the common tramp, can in no wise explain to itself the gaiety of these passers-by. I knew one man who was arrested as a runaway lunatic, because although a full-grown person with a red beard, he skipped as he went like a child. And you would be astonished if I were to tell you all the grave and learned heads who have confessed to me that, when on walking tours, they sang—and sang very ill—and had a pair of red ears when, as described above, the inauspicious peasant plumped into their arms from round a corner. And here, lest you should think I am exaggerating, is Hazlitt's own confession, from his essay *On Going a Journey*, which is so good that there should be a tax levied on all who have not read it:—

"Give me the clear blue sky over my head," says he, "and the green turf beneath my feet, a winding road before me, and a three hours' march to dinner—and then to thinking!

It is hard if I cannot start some game on these lone heaths. I laugh, I run, I leap, I sing for joy."

Bravo! After that adventure of my friend with the policeman, you would not have cared, would you, to publish that in the first person? But we have no bravery nowadays, and, even in books, must all pretend to be as dull and foolish as our neighbours. It was not so with Hazlitt. And notice how learned he is (as, indeed, throughout the essay) in the theory of walking tours. He is none of your athletic men in purple stockings, who walk their fifty miles a day: three hours' march is his ideal. And then he must have a winding road, the epicure!

Yet there is one thing I object to in these words of his, one thing in the great master's practice that seems to me not wholly wise. I do not approve of that leaping and running. Both of these hurry the respiration; they both shake up the brain out of its glorious open-air confusion; and they both break the pace. Uneven walking is not so agreeable to the body, and it distracts and irritates the mind. Whereas, when once you have fallen into an equable stride, it requires no conscious thought from you to keep it up, and yet it prevents you from thinking earnestly of anything else. Like knitting, like the work of a copying clerk, it gradually neutralises and sets to sleep the serious activity of the mind. We can think of this or that, lightly and laughingly, as a child thinks, or as we think in a morning doze; we can make puns or puzzle out acrostics, and trifle in a thousand ways with words and rhymes; but when it comes to honest work, when we come to gather ourselves together for an effort, we may sound the trumpet as loud and long as we please; the great barons of the mind will not rally to the standard, but sit, each one, at home, warming his hands over his own fire and brooding on his own private thought!

In the course of a day's walk, you see, there is much variance in the mood. From the exhilaration of the start, to the happy phlegm of the arrival, the change is certainly great. As the day goes on, the traveller moves from the one extreme towards the other. He becomes more and more incorporated with the material landscape, and the open-air drunkenness grows upon him with great strides, until he posts along the road, and sees everything about him, as in a cheerful dream. The first is certainly brighter, but the second stage is the more peaceful. A man does not make so many articles towards the end, nor does he laugh aloud; but the purely animal pleasures, the sense of physical wellbeing, the delight of every inhalation, of every time the muscles tighten down the thigh, console him for the absence of the others, and bring him to his destination still content.

Nor must I forget to say a word on bivouacs. You come to a milestone on a hill, or some place where deep ways meet under trees; and off goes the knapsack, and down you sit to smoke a pipe in the shade. You sink into yourself, and the birds come round and look at you; and your smoke dissipates upon the afternoon under the blue dome of heaven; and the sun lies warm upon your feet, and the cool air visits your neck and turns aside your open shirt. If you are not happy, you must have an evil conscience. You may dally as long as you like by the roadside. It is almost as if the millennium were arrived, when we shall throw our clocks and watches over the housetop, and remember time and seasons no more. Nor to keep hours for a lifetime is, I was going to say, to live for ever. You have no idea, unless you have tried it, how endlessly long is a summer's day, that you measure out only by hunger, and bring to an end only when you are drowsy. I know a village where there are hardly any clocks, where no one knows more of the days of the week than by a sort of instinct for the fête on Sundays, and where only one person can tell you the day of the month, and she is generally wrong; and if people were aware how slow Time journeyed in that village, and what armfuls of spare hours he gives, over and above the bargain, to its wise inhabitants, I believe there would be a stampede out of London, Liverpool, Paris, and a variety of large towns, where the clocks lose their heads, and shake the hours out each one faster than the other, as though they were all in a wager. And all these foolish pilgrims would each bring his own misery along with him, in a watch-pocket! It is to be noticed, there were no clocks and watches in the much-vaunted days before the flood. It follows, of course, there were no appointments, and punctuality was not yet thought upon. "Though ye take from a covetous man all his treasure," says Milton, "he has yet one jewel left; ye cannot deprive him of his covetousness." And so I would say of a modern man of business, you may do what you will for him, put him in Eden, give him the elixir of life—he has still a flaw at heart, he still has his business habits. Now, there is no time when business habits are more mitigated than on a walking tour. And so during these halts, as I say, you will feel almost free.

But it is at night, and after dinner, that the best hour comes. There are no such pipes to be smoked as those that follow a good day's march; the flavour of the tobacco is a thing to be remembered, it is so dry and aromatic, so full and so fine. If you wind up the evening with grog, you will own there was never such grog; at every sip a jocund tranquillity spreads about your limbs and sits easily in your heart. If you read a book—and you will never do so save by fits and starts—you find the language strangely racy and harmonious; words take a new meaning; single sentences possess the ear for half-an-hour together; and the writer endears himself to you, at every page, by the nicest coincidence of sentiment. It seems as if it were a book you had written yourself in a dream. To all we have read on such occasions we look back with special favour. "It was on the 10th of April, 1798," says Hazlitt, with amorous precision, "that I sat down to a volume of the new *Héloïse*, at the Inn at Llangollen, over a bottle of sherry and a cold chicken." I should wish to quote more, for though we are mighty fine fellows nowadays, we cannot write like Hazlitt. And, talking of that, a volume of Hazlitt's essays would be a capital pocket-book on such a journey; so would a volume of Heine's songs; and for *Tristram Shandy* I can pledge a fair experience.

If the evening be fine and warm, there is nothing better in life than to lounge before the inn door in the sunset, or lean over the parapet of the bridge, to watch the weeds and the quick fishes. It is then, if ever, that you taste Joviality to the full significance of that audacious word. Your muscles are so agreeably slack, you feel so clean and so strong and so idle, that whether you move or sit still, whatever you do is done with pride and a kingly sort of pleasure. You fall in talk with any one, wise or foolish, drunk or sober. And it seems as if a hot walk purged you, more than of anything else, of all narrowness and pride, and left curiosity to play its part freely, as in a child or a man of science. You lay aside all your own hobbies, to watch provincial humours develop themselves before you, now as a laughable farce, and now grave and beautiful like an old tale.

Or perhaps you are left to your own company for the night, and surly weather imprisons you by the fire. You may remember how Burns, numbering past pleasures, dwells upon the hours when he has been "happy thinking." It is a phrase that may well perplex a poor modern, girt about on every side by clocks and chimes, and haunted, even at night, by flaming dial-plates. For we are all so busy, and have so many far-off projects to realise, and castles in the fire to turn into solid habitable mansions on a gravel soil, that we can find no time for pleasure trips into the Land of Thought and among the Hills of Vanity. Changed times, indeed, when we must sit all night, beside the fire, with folded hands; and a changed world for most of us, when we find we can pass the hours without discontent, and be happy thinking. We are in such haste to be doing, to be writing, to be gathering gear, to make our voice audible a moment in the derisive silence of eternity, that we forget that one thing, of which these are but the parts—namely, to live. We fall in love, we drink hard, we run to and fro upon the earth like frightened sheep. And now you are to ask yourself if, when all is done, you would not have been better to sit by the fire at home and be happy thinking. To sit still and contemplate,—to remember the faces of women without desire, to be pleased by the great deeds of men without envy, to be everything and everywhere in sympathy, and yet content to remain where and what you are—is not this to know both wisdom and virtue, and to dwell with happiness? After all, it is not they who carry flags, but they who look upon it from a private chamber, who have the fun of the procession. And once you are at that, you are in the very humour of all social heresy. It is no time for shuffling, or for big, empty words. If you ask yourself what you mean by fame, riches, or learning, the answer is far to seek; and you go back into that kingdom of light imaginations, which seem so vain in the eyes of Philistines perspiring after wealth, and so momentous to those who are stricken with the disproportions of the world, and, in the face of the gigantic stars, cannot stop to split differences between two degrees of the infinitesimally small, such as a tobacco-pipe or the Roman Empire, a million of money or a fiddlestick's end.

You lean from the window, your last pipe reeking whitely into the darkness, your body full of delicious pains, your mind enthroned in the seventh circle of content; when suddenly the mood changes, the weather-cock goes about, and you ask yourself one question more: whether, for the interval, you have been the wisest philosopher or the most egregious of donkeys? Human experience is not yet able to reply; but at least you have had a fine moment, and looked down upon all the kingdoms of the earth. And whether it was wise or foolish, to-morrow's travel will carry you, body and mind, into some different parish of the infinite.

A NIGHT AMONG THE PINES

FROM Bleymard after dinner, although it was already late, I set out to scale a portion of the Lozère. An ill-marked stony drove-road guided me forward; and I met nearly half-a-dozen bullock-carts descending from the woods, each laden with a whole pine-tree for the winter's firing. At the top of the woods, which do not climb very high upon this cold ridge, I struck leftward by a path among the pines, until I hit on a dell of green turf, where a streamlet made a little spout over some stones to serve me for a water-tap. "In a more sacred or sequestered bower . . . nor nymph nor faunus haunted." The trees were not old, but they grew thickly round the glade: there was no outlook, except north-eastward upon distant hill-tops, or straight upward to the sky; and the encampment felt secure and private like a room. By the time I had made my arrangements and fed Modestine, the day was already beginning to decline. I buckled myself to the knees into my sack and made a hearty meal; and as soon as the sun went down, I pulled my cap over my eyes and fell asleep.

Night is a dead monotonous period under a roof; but in the open world it passes lightly, with its stars and dews and perfumes, and the hours are marked by changes in the face of Nature. What seems a kind of temporal death to people choked between walls and curtains, is only a light and living slumber to the man who sleeps afield. All night long he can hear Nature breathing deeply and freely; even as she takes her rest, she turns and smiles; and there is one stirring hour unknown to those who dwell in houses, when a wakeful influence goes abroad over the sleeping hemisphere, and all the outdoor world are on their feet. It is then that the cock first crows, not this time to announce the dawn, but like a cheerful watchman speeding the course of night. Cattle awake on the meadows; sheep break their fast on dewy hillsides, and change to a new lair among the ferns; and houseless men, who have lain down with the fowls, open their dim eyes and behold the beauty of the night.

At what inaudible summons, at what gentle touch of Nature, are all these sleepers thus recalled in the same hour to life? Do the stars rain down an influence, or do we share some thrill of mother earth below our resting bodies? Even shepherds and old countryfolk, who are the deepest read in these arcana, have not a guess as to the means or purpose of this nightly resurrection. Towards two in the morning they declare the thing takes place; and neither know nor inquire further. And at least it is a pleasant incident. We are disturbed in our slumber only, like the luxurious Montaigne, "that we may the better and more sensibly relish it." We have a moment to look upon the stars. And there is a special pleasure for some minds in the reflection that we share the impulse with all outdoor creatures in our neighbourhood, that we have escaped out of the Bastille of civilisation, and are become, for the time being, a mere kindly animal and a sheep of Nature's flock.

When the hour came to me among the pines, I wakened thirsty. My tin was standing by me half full of water. I emptied it at a draught; and feeling broad awake after this internal cold aspersion, sat upright to make a cigarette. The stars were clear, coloured, and jewel-like, but not frosty. A faint silvery vapour stood for the Milky Way. All around me the black fir-points stood upright and stock-still. By the whiteness of the pack-saddle, I could see Modestine walking round and round at the length of her tether; I could hear her steadily munching at the sward; but there was not another sound, save the indescribable quiet talk of the runnel over the stones. I lay lazily smoking and studying the colour of the sky, as we call the void of space, from where it showed a reddish grey behind the pines to where it showed a glossy blue-black between the stars. As if to be more like a pedlar, I wear a silver ring. This I could see faintly shining as I raised or lowered the cigarette; and at each whiff the inside of my hand was illuminated, and became for a second the highest light in the landscape.

A faint wind, more like a moving coolness than a stream of air, passed down the glade from time to time; so that even in my great chamber the air was being renewed all night long. I thought with horror of the inn at Chasseradès and the congregated nightcaps; with horror of the nocturnal prowesses of clerks and students, of hot theatres and pass-keys and close rooms. I have not often enjoyed a more serene possession of myself, nor felt more independent of material aids. The outer world, from which we cower into our houses, seemed after all a gentle habitable place; and night after night a man's bed, it seemed, was laid and waiting for him in the fields, where God keeps an open house. I thought I had rediscovered one of those truths which are revealed to savages and hid from political economists: at the least, I had discovered a new pleasure for myself. And yet even while I was exulting in my solitude I became aware of a strange lack. I wished a companion to lie near me in the starlight, silent and not moving, but ever within touch. For there is a fellowship more quiet even than solitude, and which, rightly understood, is solitude made perfect. And to live out of doors with the woman a man loves is of all lives the most complete and free.

As I thus lay, between content and longing, a faint noise stole towards me through the pines. I thought, at first, it was the crowing of cocks or the barking of dogs at some very distant farm; but steadily and gradually it took articulate shape in my ears, until I became aware that a passenger was going by upon the high-road in the valley, and singing loudly as he went. There was more of good-will than grace in his performance; but he trolled with ample lungs; and the sound of his voice took hold upon the hillside and set the air shaking in the leafy glens. I have heard people passing by night in sleeping cities; some of them sang; one, I remember, played loudly on the bagpipes. I have heard the rattle of a cart or carriage spring up suddenly after hours of stillness, and pass, for some minutes, within the range of my hearing as I lay abed. There is a romance about all who are abroad in the black hours, and with something of a thrill we try to guess their business. But here the romance was double: first, this glad passenger, lit internally with wine, who sent up his voice in music through the night; and then I, on the other hand, buckled into my sack, and smoking alone in the pinewoods between four and five thousand feet towards the stars.

When I awoke again (Sunday, 29th September), many of the stars had disappeared; only the stronger companions of the night still burned visibly overhead; and away towards the east I saw a faint haze of light upon the horizon, such as had been the Milky Way when I was last awake. Day was at hand. I lit my lantern, and by its glow-worm light put on my boots and gaiters; then I broke up some bread for Modestine, filled my can at the water-tap, and lit my spirit-lamp to boil myself some chocolate. The blue darkness lay long in the glade where I had so sweetly slumbered; but soon there was a broad streak of orange melting into gold along the mountain-tops of Vivarais. A solemn glee possessed my mind at this gradual and lovely coming in of day. I heard the runnel with delight; I looked round me for something beautiful and unexpected; but the still black pine-trees, the hollow glade, the munching ass, remained unchanged in figure. Nothing had altered but the light, and that, indeed, shed over all a spirit of life and of breathing peace, and moved me to a strange exhilaration.

I drank my water-chocolate, which was hot if it was not rich, and strolled here and there, and up and down about the glade. While I was thus delaying, a gush of steady wind, as long as a heavy sigh, poured direct out of the quarter of the morning. It was cold, and set me sneezing. The trees near at hand tossed their black plumes in its passage; and I could see the thin distant spires of pine along the edge of the hill rock slightly to and fro against the golden east. Ten minutes after, the sunlight spread at a gallop along the hillside, scattering shadows and sparkles, and the day had come completely.

I hastened to prepare my pack, and tackle the steep ascent that lay before me; but I had something on my mind. It was only a fancy; yet a fancy will sometimes be importunate. I had been most hospitably received and punctually served in my green caravanserai. The room was airy, the water excellent, and the dawn had called me to a moment. I say nothing of the tapestries or the inimitable ceiling, nor yet of the view which I commanded from the windows; but I felt I was in some one's debt for all this liberal entertainment. And so it pleased me, in a half-laughing way, to leave pieces of money on the turf as I went along, until I had left enough for my night's lodging. I trust they did not fall to some rich and churlish drover.

FOREST NOTES

ON THE PLAIN

PERHAPS the reader knows already the aspect of the great levels of the Gâtinais, where they border with the wooded hills of Fontainebleau. Here and there a few grey rocks creep out of the forest as if to sun themselves. Here and there a few apple-trees stand together on a knoll. The quaint, undignified tartan of a myriad small fields dies out into the distance; the strips blend and disappear; and the dead flat lies forth open and empty, with no accident save perhaps a thin line of trees or faint church spire against the sky. Solemn and vast at all times, in spite of pettiness in the near details, the impression becomes more solemn and vast towards evening. The sun goes down, a swollen orange, as it were into the sea. A blue-clad peasant rides home, with a harrow smoking behind him among the dry clods. Another still works with his wife in their little strip. An immense shadow fills the plain; these people stand in it up to their shoulders; and their heads, as they stoop over their work and rise again, are relieved from time to time against the golden sky.

These peasant farmers are well off nowadays, and not by any means overworked; but somehow you always see in them the historical representative of the serf of yore, and think not so much of present times, which may be prosperous enough, as of the old days when the peasant was taxed beyond possibility of payment, and lived, in Michelet's image, like a hare between two furrows. These very people now weeding their patch under the broad sunset, that very man and his wife, it seems to us, have suffered all the wrongs of France. It is they who have been their country's scapegoat for long ages; they who, generation after generation, have sowed and not reaped, reaped and another has garnered; and who have now entered into their reward, and enjoy their good things in their turn. For the days are gone by when the Seigneur ruled and profited. "Le Seigneur," says the old formula, "enferme ses manants comme sous porte et gonds, du ciel à la terre. Tout est à lui, forêt chenue, oiseau dans l'air, poisson dans l'eau, bête au buisson, l'onde qui coule, la cloche dont le son au loin roule." Such was his old state of sovereignty, a local god rather than a mere king. And now you may ask yourself where he is, and look round for vestiges of my late lord, and in all the country-side there is no trace of him but his forlorn and fallen mansion. At the end of a long avenue, now sown with grain, in the midst of a close full of cypresses and lilacs, ducks and crowing chanticleers and droning bees, the old château lifts its red chimneys and peaked roofs and turning vanes into the wind and sun. There is a glad spring bustle in the air, perhaps, and the lilacs are all in flower, and the creepers green about the broken balustrade: but no spring shall revive the honour of the place. Old women of the people, little children of the people, saunter and gambol in the walled court or feed the ducks in the neglected moat. Plough-horses, mighty of limb, browse in the long stables. The dial-hand on the clock waits for some better hour. Out on the plain, where hot sweat trickles into men's eyes, and the spade goes in deep and comes up slowly, perhaps the peasant may feel a movement of joy at his heart when he thinks that these spacious chimneys are now cold, which have so often blazed and flickered upon gay folk at supper, while he and his hollow-eyed children watched through the night with empty bellies and cold feet. And perhaps, as he raises his head and sees the forest lying like a coast-line of low hills along the sea-level of the plain, perhaps forest and château hold no unsimilar place in his affections.

If the château was my lord's, the forest was my lord the king's; neither of them for this poor Jacques. If he thought to eke out his meagre way of life by some petty theft of wood for the fire, or for a new roof-tree, he found himself face to face with a whole department, from the Grand Master of the Woods and Waters, who was a high-born lord, down to the common sergeant, who was a peasant like himself, and wore stripes or a bandoleer by way of uniform. For the first offence, by the Salic law, there was a fine of fifteen sols; and should a man be taken more than once in fault, or circumstances aggravate the colour of his guilt, he might be whipped, branded, or hanged. There was a hangman over at Melun, and, I doubt not, a fine tall gibbet hard by the town gate, where Jacques might see his fellows dangle against the sky as he went to market.

And then, if he lived near to a cover, there would be the more hares and rabbits to eat out his harvest, and the more hunters to trample it down. My lord has a new horn from England. He has laid out seven francs in decorating it with silver and gold, and fitting it with a silken leash to hang about his shoulder. The hounds have been on a pilgrimage to the shrine of Saint Mesmer, or Saint Hubert in the Ardennes, or some other holy intercessor who has made a speciality of the health of hunting-dogs. In the grey dawn the game was turned and the branch broken by our best piqueur. A rare day's hunting lies before us. Wind a jolly flourish, sound the *bien-aller* with all your lungs. Jacques must stand by, hat in hand, while the quarry and hound and huntsman sweep across his field, and a year's sparing and labouring is as though it had not been. If he can see the ruin with a good enough grace, who knows but he may fall in favour with my lord; who knows but his son may become the last and least among the servants at his lordship's kennel—one of the two poor varlets who get no wages and sleep at night among the hounds?[1]

For all that, the forest has been of use to Jacques, not only warming him with fallen wood, but giving him shelter in days of sore trouble, when my lord of the château, with all his troopers and trumpets, had been beaten from field after field into some ultimate fastness, or lay over-seas in an English prison. In these dark days, when the watch on the church steeple saw the smoke of burning villages on the sky-line, or a clump of spears and fluttering pennons drawing nigh across the plain, these good folk gat them up, with all their household gods, into the wood, whence, from some high spur, their timid scouts might overlook the coming and going of the marauders, and see the harvest ridden down, and church and cottage go up to heaven all night in flame. It was but an un-homely refuge that the woods afforded, where they must abide all change of weather and keep house with wolves and vipers. Often there was none left alive, when they returned, to show the old divisions of field from field. And yet, as times went, when the wolves entered at night into depopulated Paris, and perhaps De Retz was passing by with a company of demons like himself, even in these caves and thickets there were glad hearts and grateful prayers.

Once or twice, as I say, in the course of the ages, the forest may have served the peasant well, but at heart it is a royal forest, and noble by old associations. These woods have rung to the horns of all the kings of France, from Philip Augustus downwards. They have seen Saint Louis exercise the dogs he brought with him from Egypt; Francis I. go a-hunting with ten thousand horses in his train; and Peter of Russia following his first stag. And so they are still haunted for the imagination by royal hunts and progresses, and peopled with the faces of memorable men of yore. And this distinction is not only in virtue of the pastime of dead monarchs. Great events, great revolutions, great cycles in the affairs of men, have here left their note, here taken shape in some significant and dramatic situation. It was hence that Guise and his leaguers led Charles the Ninth a prisoner to Paris. Here, booted and spurred, and with all his dogs about him, Napoleon met the Pope beside a woodland cross. Here, on his way to Elba not so long after, he kissed the eagle of the Old Guard, and spoke words of passionate farewell to his soldiers. And here, after Waterloo, rather than yield its ensign to the new power, one of his faithful regiments burned that memorial of so much toil and glory on the Grand Master's table, and drank its dust in brandy, as a devout priest consumes the remnants of the Host.

IDLE HOURS

The woods by night, in all their uncanny effect, are not rightly to be understood until you can compare them with the woods by day. The stillness of the medium, the floor of glittering sand, these trees that go streaming up like monstrous sea-weeds and waver in the moving winds like the weeds in submarine currents, all these set the mind working on the thought of what you may have seen off a foreland or over the side of a boat, and make you feel like a diver, down in the quiet water, fathoms below the tumbling, transitory surface of the sea. And yet in itself, as I say, the strangeness of these nocturnal solitudes is not to be felt fully without the sense of contrast. You must have risen in the morning and seen the woods as they are by day, kindled and coloured in the sun's light; you must have felt the odour of innumerable trees at even, the unsparing heat along the forest roads, and the coolness of the groves.

And on the first morning you will doubtless rise betimes. If you have not been wakened before by the visit of some adventurous pigeon, you will be wakened as soon as the sun can reach your window—for there are no blinds or shutters to keep him out—and the room, with its bare wood floor and bare whitewashed walls, shines all round you in a sort of glory of reflected lights. You may doze a while longer by snatches, or lie awake to study the charcoal men and dogs and horses with which former occupants have defiled the partitions: Thiers, with wily profile; local celebrities, pipe in hand; or, maybe, a romantic landscape splashed in oil. Meanwhile artist after artist drops into the salle-à-manger for coffee, and then shoulders easel, sunshade, stool, and paint-box, bound into a fagot, and sets off for what he calls his "motive." And artist after artist, as he goes out of the village, carries with him a little following of dogs. For the dogs, who belong only nominally to any special master, hang about the gate of the forest all day long, and whenever any one goes by who hits their fancy, profit by his escort, and go forth with him to play an hour or two at hunting. They would like to be under the trees all day. But they cannot go alone. They require a pretext. And so they take the passing artist as an excuse to go into the woods, as they might take a walking-stick as an excuse to bathe. With quick ears, long spines, and bandy legs, or perhaps as tall as a greyhound and with a bulldog's head, this company of mongrels will trot by your side all day and come home with you at night, still showing white teeth and wagging stunted tail. Their good humour is not to be exhausted. You may pelt them with stones if you please, and all they will do is to give you a wider berth. If once they come out with you, to you they will remain faithful, and with you return; although if you meet them next morning in the street, it is as like as not they will cut you with a countenance of brass.

The forest—a strange thing for an Englishman—is very destitute of birds. This is no country where every patch of wood among the meadows gibes up an increase of song, and every valley wandered through by a streamlet rings and reverberates from side to side with a profusion of clear notes. And this rarity of birds is not to be regretted on its own account only. For the insects prosper in their absence, and become as one of the plagues of Egypt. Ants swarm in the hot sand; mosquitoes drone their nasal drone; wherever the sun finds a hole in the roof of the forest, you see a myriad transparent creatures coming and going in the shaft of light; and even between-whiles, even where there is no incursion of sun-rays into the dark arcade of the wood, you are conscious of a continual drift of insects, an ebb and flow of infinitesimal living things between the trees. Nor are insects the only evil creatures that haunt the forest. For you may plump into a cave among the rocks, and find yourself face to face with a wild boar, or see a crooked viper slither across the road.

Perhaps you may set yourself down in the bay between two spreading beech-roots with a book on your lap, and be awakened all of a sudden by a friend: "I say, just keep where you are, will you? You make the jolliest motive." And you reply: "Well, I don't mind, if I may smoke." And thereafter the hours go idly by. Your friend at the easel labours doggedly a little way off, in the wide shadow of the tree; and yet farther, across a strait of glaring sunshine, you see another painter, encamped in the shadow of another tree, and up to his waist in the fern. You cannot watch your own effigy growing out of the white trunk, and the trunk beginning to stand forth from the rest of the wood, and the whole picture getting dappled over with the flecks of sun that slip through the leaves overhead, and, as a wind goes by and sets the trees a-talking, flicker hither and thither like butterflies of light. But you know it is going forward; and, out of emulation with the painter, get ready your own palette, and lay out the colour for a woodland scene in words.

Your tree stands in a hollow paved with fern and heather, set in a basin of low hills, and scattered over with rocks and junipers. All the open is steeped in pitiless sunlight. Everything stands out as though it were cut in cardboard, every colour is strained into its highest key. The boulders are some of them upright and dead like monolithic castles, some of them prone like sleeping cattle. The junipers—looking, in their soiled and ragged mourning, like some funeral procession that has gone seeking the place of sepulchre three hundred years and more in wind and rain—are daubed in forcibly against the glowing ferns and heather. Every tassel of their rusty foliage is defined with pre-Raphaelite minuteness. And a sorry figure they make out there in the sun, like misbegotten yew-trees! The scene is all pitched in a key of colour so peculiar, and lit up with such a discharge of violent sunlight, as a man might live fifty years in England and not see.

Meanwhile at your elbow some one tunes up a song, words of Ronsard to a pathetic tremulous air, of how the poet loved his mistress long ago, and pressed on her the flight of time, and told her how white and quiet the dead lay under the stones, and how the boat dipped and pitched as the shades embarked for the passionless land. Yet a little while, sang the poet, and there shall be no more love; only to sit and remember loves that might have been. There is a falling flourish in the air that remains in the memory and comes back in incongruous places, on the seat of hansoms or in the warm bed at night, with something of a forest savour.

"You can get up now," says the painter; "I'm at the background."

And so up you get, stretching yourself, and go your way into the wood, the daylight becoming richer and more golden, and the shadows stretching farther into the open. A cool air comes along the highways, and the scents awaken. The fir-trees breathe abroad their ozone. Out of unknown thickets comes forth the soft, secret, aromatic odour of the woods, not like a smell of the free heaven, but as though court ladies, who had known these paths in ages long gone by, still walked in the summer evenings, and shed from their brocades a breath of musk or bergamot upon the woodland winds. One side of the long avenues is still kindled with the sun, the other is plunged in transparent shadow. Over the trees the west begins to burn like a furnace; and the painters gather up their chattels, and go down, by avenue or footpath, to the plain.

A PLEASURE-PARTY

As this excursion is a matter of some length, and, moreover, we go in force, we have set aside our usual vehicle, the pony-cart, and ordered a large wagonette from Lejosne's. It has been waiting for near an hour, while one went to pack a knapsack, and t'other hurried over his toilette and coffee; but now it is filled from end to end with merry folk in summer attire, the coachman cracks his whip, and amid much applause from round the inn door, off we rattle at a spanking trot. The way lies through the forest, up hill and down dale, and by beech and pine wood, in the cheerful morning sunshine. The English get down at all the ascents and walk on ahead for exercise; the French are mightily entertained at this, and keep coyly underneath the tilt. As we go we carry with us a pleasant noise of laughter and light speech, and some one will be always breaking out into a bar or two of opera bouffe. Before we get to the Route Ronde here comes Desprez, the colourman from Fontainebleau, trudging across on his weekly peddle with a case of merchandise; and it is "Desprez, leave me some malachite green"; "Desprez, leave me so much canvas"; "Desprez, leave me this, or leave me that"; M. Desprez standing the while in the sunlight with grave face and many salutations. The next interruption is more important. For some time back we have had the sound of cannon in our ears; and now, a little past Franchard, we find a mounted trooper holding a led horse, who brings the wagonette to a stand. The artillery is practising in the Quadrilateral, it appears; passage along the Route Ronde formally interdicted for the moment. There is nothing for it but to draw up at the glaring crossroads, and get down to make fun with the notorious Cocardon, the most ungainly and ill-bred dog of all the ungainly and ill-bred dogs of Barbizon, or clamber about the sandy banks. And meanwhile the Doctor, with sun umbrella, wide Panama, and patriarchal beard, is busy wheedling and (for aught the rest of us know) bribing the too facile sentry. His speech is smooth and dulcet, his manner dignified and insinuating. It is not for nothing that the Doctor has voyaged all the world over, and speaks all languages from French to Patagonian. He has not come home trom perilous journeys to be thwarted by a corporal of horse. And so we soon see the soldier's mouth relax, and his shoulders imitate a relenting heart. "*En voiture, Messieurs, Mesdames,"* sings the Doctor; and on we go again at a good round pace, for black care follows hard after us, and discretion prevails not a little over valour in some timorous spirits of the party. At any moment we may meet the sergeant, who will send us back. At any moment we may encounter a flying shell, which will send us somewhere farther off than Grez.

Grez—for that is our destination—has been highly recommended for its beauty. *"Il y a de l'eau,"* people have said, with an emphasis, as if that settled the question, which, for a French mind, I am rather led to think it does. And Grez, when we get there, is indeed a place worthy of some praise. It lies out of the forest, a cluster of houses, with an old bridge, an old castle in ruin, and a quaint old church. The inn garden descends in terraces to the river; stableyard, kailyard, orchard, and a space of lawn, fringed with rushes and embellished with a green arbour. On the opposite bank there is a reach of English-looking plain, set thickly with willows and poplars. And between the two lies the river, clear and deep, and full of reeds and floating lilies. Water-plants cluster about the starlings of the long low bridge, and stand half-way up upon the piers in green luxuriance. They catch the dipped oar with long antennae, and chequer the slimy bottom with the shadow of their leaves. And the river wanders hither and thither among the islets, and is smothered and broken up by the reeds, like an old building in the lithe, hardy arms of the climbing ivy. You may watch the box where the good man of the inn keeps fish alive for his kitchen, one oily ripple following another over the top of the yellow deal. And you can hear a splashing and a prattle of voices from the shed under the old kirk, where the village women wash and wash all day among the fish and water-lilies. It seems as if linen washed there should be specially cool and sweet.

We have come here for the river. And no sooner have we all bathed than we board the two shallops and push off gaily, and go gliding under the trees and gathering a great treasure of water-lilies. Some one sings; some trail their hands in the cool water; some lean over the gunwale to see the image of the tall poplars far below, and the shadow of the boat, with the balanced oars and their own head protruded, glide smoothly over the yellow floor of the stream. At last, the day declining—all silent and happy, and up to the knees in the wet lilies—we punt slowly back again to the landing-place beside the bridge. There is a wish for solitude on all. One hides himself in the arbour with a cigarette; another goes a walk in the country with Cocardon; a third inspects the church. And it is not till dinner is on the table, and the inn's best wine goes round from glass to glass, that we begin to throw off the restraint and fuse once more into a jolly fellowship.

Half the party are to return to-night with the wagonette; and some of the others, loath to break up good company, will go with them a bit of the way and drink a stirrup-cup at Marlotte. It is dark in the wagonette, and not so merry as it might have been. The coachman loses the road. So-and-so tries to light fireworks with the most indifferent success. Some sing, but the rest are too weary to applaud; and it seems as if the festival were fairly at an end—

> "Nous avons fait la noce,
> Rentrons ô nos foyers!"

And such is the burthen, even after we have come to Marlotte and taken our places in the court at Mother Antonine's. There is punch on the long table out in the open air, where the guests dine in summer weather. The candles flare in the night wind, and the faces round the punch are lit up, with shifting emphasis, against a background of complete and solid darkness. It is all picturesque enough; but the fact is, we are aweary. We yawn; we are out of the vein; we have made the wedding, as the song says, and now, for pleasure's sake, let's make an end on't. When here comes striding into the court, booted to mid-thigh, spurred and splashed, in a jacket of green cord, the great, famous, and redoubtable Blank; and in a moment the fire kindles again, and the night is witness of our laughter as he imitates Spaniards, Germans,

Englishmen, picture-dealers, all eccentric ways of speaking and thinking, with a possession, a fury, a strain of mind and voice, that would rather suggest a nervous crisis than a desire to please. We are as merry as ever when the trap sets forth again, and say farewell noisily to all the good folk going farther. Then, as we are far enough from thoughts of sleep, we visit Blank in his quaint house, and sit an hour or so in a great tapestried chamber, laid with furs, littered with sleeping hounds, and lit up, in fantastic shadow and shine, by a wood fire in a mediaeval chimney. And then we plod back through the darkness to the inn beside the river.

How quick bright things come to confusion! When we arise next morning, the grey showers fall steadily, the trees hang limp, and the face of the stream is spoiled with dimpling raindrops. Yesterday's lilies encumber the garden walk, or begin, dismally enough, their voyage towards the Seine and the salt sea. A sickly shimmer lies upon the dripping house-roofs, and all the colour is washed out of the green and golden landscape of last night, as though an envious man had taken a water-colour sketch and blotted it together with a sponge. We go out a-walking in the wet roads. But the roads about Grez have a trick of their own. They go on for a while among clumps of willows and patches of vine, and then, suddenly and without any warning, cease and determine in some miry hollow or upon some bald knowe;

and you have a short period of hope, then right-about face, and back the way you came! So we draw about the kitchen fire and play a round game of cards for ha'pence, or go to the billiard-room for a match at corks; and by one consent a messenger is sent over for the wagonette—Grez shall be left to-morrow.

To-morrow dawns so fair that two of the party agree to walk back for exercise, and let their knapsacks follow by the trap. I need hardly say they are neither of them French; for, of all English phrases, the phrase "for exercise" is the least comprehensible across the Straits of Dover. All goes well for a while with the pedestrians. The wet woods are full of scents in the noontide. At a certain cross, where there is a guardhouse, they make a halt, for the forester's wife is the daughter of their good host at Barbizon. And so there they are hospitably received by the comely woman, with one child in her arms and another prattling and tottering at her gown, and drink some syrup of quince in the back parlour, with a map of the forest on the wall, and some prints of love-affairs and the great Napoleon hunting. As they draw near the Quadrilateral, and hear once more the report of the big guns, they take a by-road to avoid the sentries, and go on a while somewhat vaguely, with the sound of the cannon in their ears and the rain beginning to fall. The ways grow wider and sandier; here and there there are real sand-hills, as though by the sea-shore; the firwood is open and grows in clumps upon the hillocks, and the race of sign-posts is no more. One begins to look at the other doubtfully. "I am sure we should keep more to the right," says one; and the other is just as certain they should hold to the left. And now, suddenly, the heavens open, and the rain falls "sheer and strong and loud," as out of a shower-bath. In a moment they are as wet as shipwrecked sailors. They cannot see out of their eyes for the drift, and the water churns and gurgles in their boots. They leave the track and try across country with a gambler's desperation, for it seems as if it were impossible to make the situation worse; and, for the next hour, go scrambling from boulder to boulder, or plod along paths that are now no more than rivulets, and across waste clearings where the scattered shells and broken fir-trees tell all too plainly of the cannon in the distance. And meantime the cannon grumble out responses to the grumbling thunder. There is such a mixture of melodrama and sheer discomfort about all this, it is at once so grey and so lurid, that it is far more agreeable to read and write about by the chimney-corner than to suffer in the person. At last they chance on the right path, and make Franchard in the early evening, the sorriest pair of wanderers that ever welcomed English ale. Thence, by the Bois d'Hyver the Ventes-Alexandre, and the Pins Brulés, to the clean hostelry, dry clothes, and dinner.

THE WOODS IN SPRING

I think you will like the forest best in the sharp early springtime, when it is just beginning to reawaken, and innumerable violets peep from among the fallen leaves; when two or three people at most sit down to dinner, and, at table, you will do well to keep a rug about your knees, for the nights are chill, and the salle-à-manger opens on the court. There is less to distract the attention, for one thing, and the forest is more itself. It is not bedotted with artists' sunshades as with unknown mushrooms, nor bestrewn with the remains of English picnics. The hunting still goes on, and at any moment your heart may be brought into your mouth as you hear far-away horns; or you may be told by an agitated peasant that the Vicomte has gone up the avenue, not ten minutes since, "*à fond de train, monsieur, et avec douze, piqueurs.*"

If you go up to some coign of vantage in the system of low hills that permeates the forest, you will see many different tracts of country, each of its own cold and melancholy neutral tint, and all mixed together and mingled the one into the other at the seams. You will see tracts of leafless beeches of a faint yellowish grey, and leafless oaks a little ruddier in the hue. Then zones of pines of a solemn green; and, dotted among the pines, or standing by themselves in rocky clearings, the delicate, snow-white trunks of birches, spreading out into snow-white branches yet more delicate, and crowned and canopied with a purple haze of twigs. And then a long, bare ridge of tumbled boulders, with bright sand-breaks between them, and wavering sandy roads among the bracken and brown heather. It is all rather cold and un-homely. It has not the perfect beauty, nor the gemlike colouring, of the wood in the later year, when it is no more than one vast colonnade of verdant shadow, tremulous with insects, intersected here and there by lanes of sunlight set in purple heather. The loveliness of the woods in March is not, assuredly, of this blowzy rustic type. It is made sharp with a grain of salt, with a touch of ugliness. It has a sting like the sting of bitter ale; you acquire the love of it as men acquire a taste for olives. And the wonderful clear, pure air wells into your lungs the while by voluptuous inhalations, and makes the eyes bright, and sets the heart tinkling to a new tune—or, rather, to an old tune; for you remember in your boyhood something akin to this spirit of adventure, this thirst for exploration, that now takes you masterfully by the hand, plunges you into many a deep grove, and drags you over many a stony crest. It is as if the whole wood were full of friendly voices calling you farther in, and you turn from one side to another, like Buridan's donkey, in a maze of pleasure.

Comely beeches send up their white, straight, clustered

branches, barred with green moss, like so many fingers from a half-clenched hand. Mighty oaks stand to the ankles in a fine tracery of underwood; thence the tall shaft climbs upwards, and the great forest of stalwart boughs spreads out into the golden evening sky, where the rooks are flying and calling. On the sward of the Bois d'Hyver the firs stand well asunder with outspread arms, like fencers saluting; and the air smells of resin all around, and the sound of the axe is rarely still. But strangest of all, and in appearance oldest of all, are the dim and wizard upland districts of young wood. The ground is carpeted with fir-tassel, and strewn with fir-apples and flakes of fallen bark. Rocks lie crouching in the thicket, guttered with rain, tufted with lichen, white with years and the rigours of the changeful seasons. Brown and yellow butterflies are sown and carried away again by the light air—like thistledown. The loneliness of these coverts is so excessive, that there are moments when pleasure draws to the verge of fear. You listen and listen for some noise to break the silence, till you grow half mesmerised by the intensity of the strain; your sense of your own identity is troubled; your brain reels, like that of some gymnosophist poring on his own nose in Asiatic jungles; and should you see your own outspread feet, you see them, not as anything of yours, but as a feature of the scene around you.

Still the forest is always, but the stillness is not always

unbroken. You can hear the wind pass in the distance over the tree-tops; sometimes briefly, like the noise of a train; sometimes with a long, steady rush, like the breaking of waves. And sometimes, close at hand, the branches move, a moan goes through the thicket, and the wood thrills to its heart. Perhaps you may hear a carriage on the road to Fontainbleau, a bird gives a dry continual chirp, the dead leaves rustle underfoot, or you may time your steps to the steady recurrent strokes of the woodman's axe. From time to time, over the low grounds, a flight of rooks goes by; and from time to time the cooing of wild doves falls upon the ear, not sweet and rich and near at hand as in England, but a sort of voice of the woods, thin and far away, as fits these solemn places. Or you hear suddenly the hollow, eager, violent barking of dogs; scared deer flit past you through the fringes of the wood; then a man or two running, in green blouse, with gun and game-bag on a bandoleer; and then, out of the thick of the trees, comes the jar of rifle shots. Or perhaps the hounds are out, and horns are blown, and scarlet-coated huntsmen flash through the clearings, and the solid noise of horses galloping passes below you, where you sit perched among the rocks and heather. The boar is afoot, and all over the forest, and in all neighbouring villages, there is a vague excitement and a vague hope; for who knows whither the chase may lead? and even to have seen a single piqueur, or spoken to a single sportsman, is to be a man of consequence for the night.

Besides men who shoot and men who ride with the hounds, there are few people in the forest, in the early spring, save woodcutters plying their axes steadily, and old women and children gathering wood for the fire. You may meet such a party coming home in the twilight; the old woman laden with a fagot of chips, and the little ones hauling a long branch behind them in her wake. That is the worst of what there is to encounter; and if I tell you of what once happened to a friend of mine, it is by no means to tantalise you with false hopes; for the adventure was unique. It was on a very cold, still, sunless morning, with a flat grey sky and a frosty tingle in the air, that this friend (who shall here be nameless) heard the notes of a key-bugle played with much hesitation, and saw the smoke of a fire spread out along the green pine-tops, in a remote uncanny glen, hard by a hill of naked boulders. He drew near warily, and beheld a picnic party seated under a tree in an open. The old father knitted a sock, the mother sat staring at the fire. The eldest son, in the uniform of a private of dragoons, was choosing out notes on a key-bugle. Two or three daughters lay in the neighbourhood picking violets. And the whole party as grave and silent as the woods around them! My friend watched for a long time, he says; but all held their peace; not one spoke or smiled; only the dragoon kept choosing out single notes upon the bugle, and the father knitted away at his work and made strange movements the while with his flexible eyebrows. They took no notice whatever of my friend's presence, which was disquieting in itself, and increased the resemblance of the whole party to mechanical waxworks. Certainly, he affirms, a wax figure might have played the bugle with more spirit than that strange dragoon. And as this hypothesis of his became more certain, the awful insolubility of why they should be left out there in the woods with nobody to wind them up again when they ran down, and a growing disquietude as to what might happen next, became too much for his courage, and he turned tail, and fairly took to his heels. It might have been a singing in his ears, but he fancies he was followed as he ran by a peal of Titanic laughter. Nothing has ever transpired to clear up the mystery; it may be they were automata; or it may be (and this is the theory to which I lean myself) that this is all another chapter of Heine's "Gods in Exile"; that the upright old man with the eyebrows was no other than Father Jove, and the young dragoon with the taste for music either Apollo or Mars.

MORALITY

Strange indeed is the attraction of the forest for the minds of men. Not one or two only, but a great chorus of grateful voices have arisen to spread abroad its fame. Half the famous writers of modern France have had their word to say about Fontainebleau. Chateaubriand, Michelet, Béranger, Georges Sand, de Senancour, Flaubert Mürger, the brothers Goncourt, Théodore de Banville, each of these has done something to the eternal praise and memory of these woods. Even at the very worst of times, even when the picturesque was anathema in the eyes of all Persons of Taste, the forest still preserved a certain reputation for beauty. It was in 1730 that the Abbé Guilbert published his *Historical Description of the Palace, Town, and Forest of Fontainebleau*. And very droll it is to see him, as he tries to set forth his admiration in terms of what was then permissible. The monstrous rocks, etc., says the Abbé, "sont admirées avec surprise des voyageurs qui s'écrient aussitôt avec Horace: Ut mihi devio rupes et vacuum nemus mirari libet." The good man is not exactly lyrical in his praise; and you see how he sets his back against Horace as against a trusty oak. Horace, at any rate, was classical. For the rest, however, the Abbé likes places where many alleys meet; or which, like the Belle-Étoile, are kept up "by a special gardener," and admires at the Table du Roi the labours of the Grand Master of Woods and Waters, the Sieur de la Falure, "qui a fait faire ce magnifique endroit."

But indeed, it is not so much for its beauty that the forest makes a claim upon men's hearts, as for that subtle something, that quality of the air, that emanation from the old trees, that so wonderfully changes and renews a weary spirit. Disappointed men, sick Francis Firsts and vanquished Grand Monarchs, time out of mind have come here for consolation. Hither perplexed folk have retired out of the press of life, as into a deep bay-window on some night of masquerade, and here found quiet and silence, and rest, the mother of wisdom. It is the great moral spa; this forest without a fountain is itself the great fountain of Juventius. It is the best place in the world to bring an old sorrow that has been a long while your friend and enemy; and if, like Béranger's, your gaiety has run away from home and left open the door for sorrow to come in, of all covers in Europe, it is here you may expect to find the truant hid. With every hour you change. The air penetrates through your clothes, and nestles to your living body. You love exercise and slumber, long fasting and full meals. You forget all your scruples and live a while in peace and freedom, and for the moment only. For here, all is absent that can stimulate to moral feeling. Such people as you see may be old, or toil-worn, or sorry; but you see them framed in the forest, like figures on a painted canvas; and for you, they are not people in any living and kindly sense. You forget the grim contrariety of interests. You forget the narrow lane where all men jostle together in unchivalrous contention, and the kennel, deep and unclean, that gapes on either hand for the defeated. Life is simple enough, it seems, and the very idea of sacrifice becomes like a mad fancy out of a last night's dream.

Your ideal is not perhaps high, but it is plain and possible. You become enamoured of a life of change and movement and the open air, where the muscles shall be more exercised than the affections. When you have had your will of the forest, you may visit the whole round world. You may buckle on your knapsack and take the road on foot. You may bestride a good nag, and ride forth, with a pair of saddle-bags, into the enchanted East. You may cross the Black Forest, and see Germany wide-spread before you, like a map, dotted with old cities, walled and spired, that dream all day on their own reflections in the Rhine or Danube. You may pass the spinal cord of Europe and go down from Alpine glaciers to where Italy extends her marble moles and glasses her marble palaces in the midland sea. You may sleep in flying trains or wayside taverns. You may be awakened at dawn by the scream of the express or the small pipe of the robin in the hedge. For you the rain should allay the dust of the beaten road; the wind dry your clothes upon you as you walked. Autumn should hang out russet pears and purple grapes along the lane; inn after inn proffer you their cups of raw wine; river by river receive your body in the sultry noon. Wherever you went warm valleys and high trees and pleasant villages should compass you about; and light fellowships should take you by the arm, and walk with you an hour upon your way.

You may see from afar off what it will come to in the end—the weather-beaten, red-nosed vagabond, consumed by a fever of the feet, cut off from all near touch of human sympathy, a waif, an Ishmael, and an outcast. And yet it will seem well—and yet, in the air of the forest, this will seem the best—to break all the network bound about your feet by birth and old companionship and loyal love, and bear your shovelful of phosphates to and fro, in town and country, until the hour of the great dissolvent.

Or, perhaps, you will keep to the cover. For the forest is by itself, and forest life owns small kinship with life in the dismal land of labour. Men are so far sophisticated that they cannot take the world as it is given to them by the sight of their eyes. Not only what they see and hear, but what they know to be behind, enter into their notion of a place. If the sea, for instance, lie just across the hills, sea-thoughts will come to them at intervals, and the tenor of their dreams from time to time will suffer a sea-change.

And so here, in this forest, a knowledge of its greatness is for much in the effect produced. You reckon up the miles that lie between you and intrusion. You may walk before you all day long, and not fear to touch the barrier of your Eden, or stumble out of fairyland into the land of gin and steam-hammers. And there is an old tale enhances for the imagination the grandeur of the woods of France, and secures you in the thought of your seclusion. When Charles VI. hunted in the time of his wild boyhood near Senlis, there was captured an old stag, having a collar of bronze about his neck, and these words engraved on the collar: "Cæsar mihi hoc donavit." It is no wonder if the minds of men were moved at this occurrence and they stood aghast to find themselves thus touching hands with forgotten ages, and following an antiquity with hound and horn. And even for you, it is scarcely in an idle curiosity that you ponder how many centuries this stag had carried its free antlers through the wood, and how many summers and winters had shone and snowed on the imperial badge. If the extent of solemn wood could thus safeguard a tall stag from the hunter's hounds and horses, might not you also play hide-and-seek, in these groves, with all the pangs and trepidations of man's life, and elude Death, the mighty hunter, for more than the span of human years? Here, also, crash his arrows; here, in the farthest glade, sounds the gallop of the pale horse. But he does not hunt this cover with all his hounds, for the game is thin and small: and if you were but alert and wary, if you lodged ever in the deepest thickets, you too might live on into later generations and astonish men by your stalwart age and the trophies of an immemorial success.

For the forest takes away from you all excuse to die. There

is nothing here to cabin or thwart your free desires. Here all the impudencies of the brawling world reach you no more. You may count your hours, like Endymion, by the strokes of the lone woodcutter, or by the progression of the lights and shadows and the sun wheeling his wide circuit through the naked heavens. Here shall you see no enemies but winter and rough weather. And if a pang comes to you at all, it will be a pang of heathful hunger. All the puling sorrows, all the carking repentance, all this talk of duty that is no duty, in the great peace, in the pure daylight of these woods, fall away from you like a garment. And if perchance you come forth upon an eminence, where the wind blows upon you large and fresh, and the pines knock their long stems together, like an ungainly sort of puppets, and see far away over the plain a factory chimney defined against the pale horizon—it is for you, as for the staid and simple peasant when, with his plough, he upturns old arms and harness from the furrow of the glebe. Ay, sure enough, there was a battle there in the old times; and, sure enough, there is a world out yonder where men strive together with a noise of oaths and weeping and clamorous dispute. So much you apprehend by an athletic act of the imagination. A faint far-off rumour as of Merovingian wars; a legend as of some dead religion.

[1] "Deux poures varlez qui n'ont nulz gages et qui gissoient

la nuit avec les chiens." See Champollion-Figeac's *Louis et Charles d'Orléans*, i. 63, and for my lord's English horn, *ibid.* 96.

Made in United States
North Haven, CT
23 October 2024